also by Harry Hill

Tim the Tiny Horse
Tim the Tiny Horse at Large
The Further Adventures of the Queen Mum
Harry Hill's Whopping Great Joke Book
Harry Hill's Bumper Book of Bloopers

HARRY HILL

A COMPLETE HISTORY OF
TIM

(the Tiny Horse)

ff
faber and faber

First published in this form in 2012
'Tim get his first taste of family life', 'Tim and George go to the park',
'Tim gets wet' and 'Tim thinks about selling out' first published in 2012
Remainder of pages 1-186 first published in 2006 as *Tim the Tiny Horse*
Remainder of pages 187-398 first published in 2008 as *Tim the Tiny Horse at Large*
by Faber and Faber Limited
Bloomsbury House, 74-77 Great Russell Street
London, WC1B 3DA

Design and colour work by Ken de Silva
Printed in the UK by CPI Group (UK) Ltd, Croydon, CR0 4YY

All rights reserved
© Harry Hill, 2006, 2008, 2012
Illustrations © Harry Hill, 2006, 2008, 2012

The right of Harry Hill to be identified as author of this work has been asserted in
accordance with Section 77 of the Copyright, Designs and Patents Act 1988

A CIP record for this book
is available from the British Library

ISBN 978-0-571-28037-7

FSC
www.fsc.org
MIX
Paper from
responsible sources
FSC® C101712

2 4 6 8 10 9 7 5 3 1

Contents

tim and the disappearing hula hoop

Tim the Tiny Horse
was tiny...

but cheerful. Here he is
playing with a 2p piece.
So you get the idea.

A sugar lump would last
him a month.

His stable was a matchbox...

with an old tic tac box
for a conservatory.

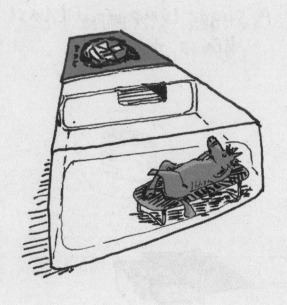

You know, somewhere
for Tim to chill out.

One fine day, Tim
the Tiny Horse went
to get his Hula Hoop
for Lunch.

It was a barbecue flavoured one
that he'd saved from a Party.

But to his horror...
it had gone!

Only a slight whiff
of barbecue sauce
lingered where once
was Tim's Hula Hoop.

Disappointed, he
wandered home,
still hungry.

Ah!

On the way, what
do you think he saw?

munch!
munch!

That's right!
A fly munching into
his very own Hula Hoop!

A fight followed.

First Tim seemed to
be winning...

then the fly seemed
to gain the upper hand.

But after about a minute
they'd both had enough...

and agreed to
Share it.

Later on, they sat down
and watched a video together.

Well, there are
no real winners in
a fight – are there?

tim gets the showbiz bug

Tim the Tiny Horse was <u>so</u> small that the blacksmith had to make his shoes from paperclips.

His saddle was made from a watch-strap.

Which is why he never wore it. Well, would you?

He was small... but he
had Standards.

Most of his activities were severely restricted. So he spent much of his time lazing in the sun.

Or watching the TV.

One day Tim the Tiny Horse sat on the patio watching the ants going about their business...

He admired their
sense of purpose.

'I need to get a job,'
he thought.

That lunchtime, as Tim sat
watching Anna Ford...

On the One O'Clock
News from the BBC,

he realised that
everyone on TV was
small...just like him.

It was perfect
for him!

Maybe he could be in a
cowboy film...

Or the Horse of the Year
Show...

or even read the lunchtime
News with Anna!

Maybe he'd meet that
special lady horse
he'd always been looking for.

He knew he shouldn't get
his hopes up as from
what he'd seen, most
of the shows on TV
were set in pubs...

and he didn't like
pubs because often
there was a dog in
there.

If There was one
thing Tim didn't like
it was **DOGS**.

Likes | Dislikes
Anna Ford | Dogs
Hula Hoops
sweets
Fly

Without further ado
Tim the Tiny Horse
set off for the TV studio.

When he arrived at the studio
everything was much bigger than
he'd been led to believe.
In fact, everything was pretty
much full size.

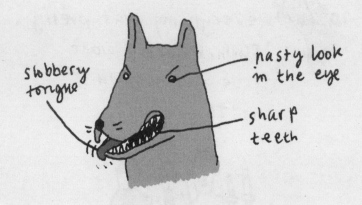

slobbery tongue

nasty look in the eye

sharp teeth

Including the dog.

'I'm not sure I want
to be a part of this,'
he thought.

And instead headed off
to the canteen...

for a sugar lump.

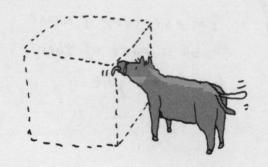

'Hmm...' thought Tim the Tiny Horse.
'The studios may not be what
I'd hoped... but the food
is first rate.'

With that, he headed for home.

After all...

there's no point in
getting a job for the
sake of it.

fly gets a girlfriend

Tim the Tiny Horse
was <u>tiny</u>.

He was so small that a pizza leaflet
would take him an hour and a half
to read...

So small was Tim that even
the small pizza was too big
for him.

What a waste of an
hour and a half.

slurp!
slurp!

No. A typical lunch
for Tim the Tiny Horse
was a Hula Hoop
(preferably barbecue beef).

One day Tim's best friend Fly
announced that he had met
a lady fly and that she was
now his 'girlfriend'.

The upshot of this was that Fly
didn't want to see Tim as much.

on a couple of occasions
Tim went round
to see if Fly wanted
to come out to play,
only to find that

Fly's girlfriend was
already there.

'What does he want?'

'Perhaps she would like
to play too,'
said Tim the Tiny Horse,
hopefully.

'I think not!' said
Fly's new girlfriend,
looking at Tim in a
way that didn't make
him feel particularly
welcome.

Tail drooping

Head held Low

Forlorn expression

Fly explained to Tim
[over the phone] that they
could still play together

but Tim should
give a little warning
before calling round.

A short time after that, Fly's
girlfriend decided she didn't
want to see Fly any more
(although they could still be
  friends).

There were no other
flies involved.

Whilst Tim was sorry to
see fly so upset...

he was secretly
pleased that things
were back to normal.

Tim felt a little bit guilty
about this feeling...

then he remembered
the look that Fly's
ex-girlfriend had given him...

and the feeling passed.

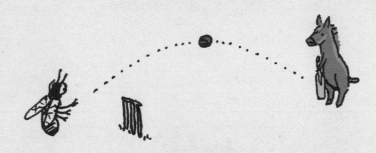

After all, you've got to stick by friends.

tim has a brush with Anna Ford

Tim the Tiny Horse was extremely small.

In fact, he was so small that he
found it difficult to get served
in bars.

Fortunately he had
a ve_ry loud voice.

N.B.
He didn't always say 'neigh'
but when he did he meant it.

Tim mainly drank shorts.

Likes	Dislikes
Anna Ford	Dogs
Hula Hoops	Fly's girlfriend
Sweets
Fly

It has been established, I think, that Tim the Tiny Horse was a great fan of the BBC News at One O'Clock... with Anna Ford.

He was fascinated by Anna
and if ever a photograph of
her appeared in the newspaper...

he would cut it out and stick
it in his scrapbook.

Once, he wrote to Anna Ford for her autograph.

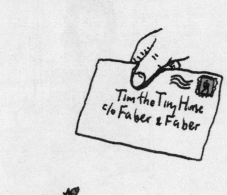

Tim the Tiny Horse
c/o Faber & Faber

After many weeks a lovely photo of Anna arrived, signed: 'To Tim, Good LUCK, Anna Ford'.

Tim the Tiny Horse pasted it on
to his bedroom wall.
He called it his Anna Ford MURAL.

Tim wrote back to Anna
asking whether it would
be possible for the two
of them to meet up.

A polite letter of refusal
came back by return of
post. It had been written
not by Anna, but by somebody
who worked with her.

For (TWO WEEKS) Tim
watched the lunchtime
news at 12·30 on ITV.

Then he went back to Anna.
Well, it doesn't do to
bear a grudge, does it?

tim and fly go out

Tim the Tiny Horse
was... well...
...very small.

To Tim a conker was a major
obstacle...

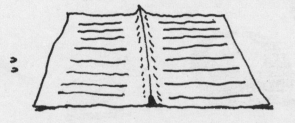

a crinkle in a piece of paper
was a real hurdle.

One day Tim and his friend
Fly decided to go to town.

TOWN 4

They set off with Fly
riding on Tim's back.

'What an adventure!'
thought Tim the Tiny Horse.
'I could buy a <u>chair</u>!'

'And I could buy some
shoes!' said Fly
out loud.

Then Tim remembered
that most chairs were
far too big for him...

...and Fly remembered that most shoes come in sets of **2** rather than **6**.

'Is this trip entirely necessary?'
said Tim the Tiny Horse.
'After all, we don't really
need anything from town.'

'Yes,' said Fly, 'and the town
is an awfully long way.'

The answer was obvious:

With that they headed home.
This time it was Tim's turn to
ride on the back of Fly.

Sometimes you're
better off just staying
<u>IN</u>

tim and fly consider the meaning of life

Tim the Tiny Horse and his best friend Fly were in the park, staring at the clouds and chatting.

'I wonder if there is such a thing as GOD,' said Fly.

'I should think so,'
said Tim the Tiny Horse.

'What about all the
bad things that happen
in the world...?'

'Like war, earthquakes and famine?' said Fly.

'Well, we've all done things
we're not proud of,'
said Tim.

And he started to
think about a grape he'd
eaten off the floor of the
supermarket without paying
for it.

At that point the sun
came out.

'Draw your own conclusion
from that!' he said,
Pointing at the sky.

Fly looked
rather sheepish.

Sometimes you have to see
the bigger picture.

tim the tiny horse logs on

Tim the Tiny Horse
was exceedingly small.

In fact, given a cocktail stick,
a piece of cotton and a hawthorn
berry...

Tim could play swingball.

lolly stick

saw here

[Having formed a bat from
a discarded lolly stick]

Tim often played his best
friend Fly at swing ball...

but rarely won as Fly would
often play the ball high.

Fly had been going on
about how his sister
had been learning at
school about the
internet...

and how fantastic
it was.

'You can look up
anything you want
and find out all
about it,'
said Fly.

so One day Tim the Tiny Horse
trotted off to the Internet Café
to log on.

However, when he got there ...

He couldn't think of
anything to look up.

So he looked hi<u>ms</u>elf up.

The internet then told him
all about a tortoise called
Tim who lived to be a hundred
and sixty years old,

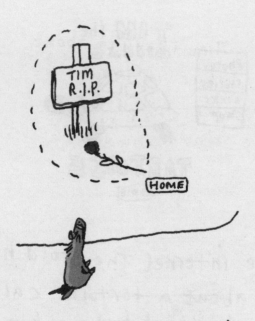

but was now dead.

Tim thought about
what it would be
like to be 160
and shuddered.

As he trotted home he thought
about his experience at the
Internet Café...

and resented the way
the internet had made him
think about something he
hadn't really wanted to
confront yet.

Ageing... and his own
mortality.

on top of that, when he
arrived home there was a
note on Tim's door from Fly,

saying that he'd called round
to see if Tim wanted to play
but Tim had been out.

It seemed the internet
wasn't as fantastic as
Tim had been led to
believe.

Author's Note: Tim always lies on his back
when particularly frustrated.

Tim Gets His First Taste of Family Life

One day it was Fly's birthday and Tim the Tiny Horse was invited round to Fly's for a birthday tea.

Fly was there, and his mum and Dad
and Fly's little sister.

Tim wished that he had a family — particularly a Mummy.

(He did in fact have a cousin in Canada)

not a birthday cake - a hat!

maple leaves

Later on, an argument
broke out between Fly
and his sister...

which quickly turned
into a fight.

'I may not have a family,'
thought Tim, 'But at least
I don't have anyone shouting
that they hate me.'

Who could possibly
hate a tiny horse?

Fly explained later that that's what <u>families</u> do sometimes.

Tim didn't really believe him —

- he'd seen the look
in her eyes - she'd
meant it alright.

'You always hurt the one
you don't like that much,'
Thought Tim the Tiny Horse.

tim does some cooking

Tim the Tiny Horse was by
no means a large horse...

but what he lacked
in the stature department
he more than made up for
in enthusiasm.

For instance, Tim was far too small to take part in the London Marathon...

[all those pounding feet would pose a real danger to him]

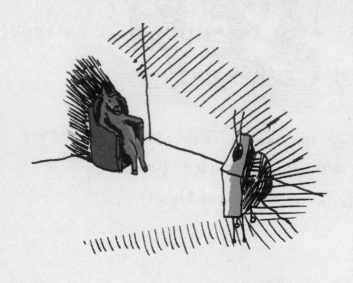

but that didn't stop him
enjoying it on the television.

One day, Tim the Tiny Horse
came upon the discarded wrapper
of a FUDGE BAR!

On closer inspection Tim realised
that there was a list of ingredients.

'The fools!'
thought Tim the Tiny Horse.
'There's nothing to stop people
from making their own fudge bars!'

Back in his kitchen he set about
making his first fudge bar.

'Let's see what I need,'
he said, reading the list of ingredients.
'Sugar... I've got that...'

'chocolate... I've got that ...'

'But what is 'non-hydrogenated
vegetable fat'?'

'Hmmm,' he thought.

'Best leave it to the experts.'

And he ate the sugar...

And the chocolate...

and with a little imagination
it tasted a bit like
...fudge!

tim goes for a job in radio

Tim the Tiny Horse was,
I'm afraid to say, a little
on the s<u>m</u>all side.

If, for instance, he was to eat
a whole Malteser...
it might take him a whole morning.
AND...

he would get a Headache
and have to spend the afternoon
in BED.

A tube of toothpaste
would last him...

well, he'd had
the same tube
for **3** years...

and there was still only a
slight dent in it.

Tim was small...
but ambitious.

One afternoon, after the News
at One O'Clock with Anna Ford,
Tim sat listening to the
cricket on the radio.

Suddenly it
dawned on him.

'Radio would be perfect
for me!' he said
out loud.

'On radio it's all in the voice.
It doesn't matter how big
you are!'

His best friend Fly told him that what he needed to do was make a 'demo' tape of his voice and send it to the people who ran the radio.

'demo', it seems, was short for

demonstration.

Tim unearthed an old
tape recorder.

'I'll be the producer,'
said FLY and pressed
the record button.

'um... er...'

Unfortunately, when put on the spot, Tim the Tiny Horse couldn't think of anything to say.

'UM... I...'

'...... hello.'

All he could manage was 'hello'.

To spare Tim any embarrassment
Fly told him there was a
'technical fault' with the tape.

They agreed that radio was
much harder than it looked.

Much easier just to
listen to it.

tim finds out that he is a winner

Tim the Tiny Horse was not
just <u>small</u> but, well, <u>tiny</u>.
(As they say, there's a clue in the name.)

He was so small he would use
a bottle-top as a hot-tub.

He had to use a cotton bud
to scrub his back.

One night, just after running his bath, the phone rang.

It was a strange man
who told Tim that he had
won a prize.

The man explained
that Tim may have
won a car, a holiday
or cash.

Immediately Tim's mind
began to race.

Clearly a car was
no good to him.

as his feet wouldn't be able
to reach the pedals...

Even if it was the car, he could always sell it and take the cash.

But a holiday, or money...

The strange man went on
to explain that, in fact, Tim
had not won the prize **yet**

but he would be put
into a prize draw.

This scared Tim
as he had once
become trapped in
a chest of drawers
as a foal.

At this point Tim looked
over at the lovely hot
steaming bath...

If he left it
much longer it
would start to
get cold.

'I think I'll give it a miss,'
said Tim the Tiny Horse
to the strange man.
'But good luck with it!'

Moments Later Tim was having
a lovely warm soak.

'Why do they always phone
at bath time?'
he wondered.

tim faces up to reality

I think we're beginning to get
the idea that in the SIZE stakes
Tim the Tiny Horse had very
little to offer.

No, he had other strengths:

Optimism...

enthusiasm...

and an interest
in current affairs...

hmm...

particularly when presented
by Anna Ford.

One night, Tim the Tiny Horse
and his best friend Fly sat
watching a television programme...

in which there were
a number of hidden
cameras...

spying on people
Living in a house.

Not a lot happened.

Fly explained
to Tim that this
was called Reality T.V.

'Reality TV would
be perfect for me!'
said Tim the Tiny Horse...

and raced towards
a dwarf cupboard...

in search of his
camcorder.

Tim set up the camcorder in his
front room ...

and filmed...

everything...

he did...

the next day.

That evening Tim the Tiny Horse
played his reality TV show
to Fly,

who fell asleep
after 5 minutes.

'Hmmm...'
thought Tim the
Tiny Horse.

YAWN

'I think this show
should be about
<u>4</u> minutes long.'

sometimes **REALITY** is better
in small doses.

tim's christmas

christmas was always
a bit quiet for tim
— being an orphan...

... and not being a particularly big fan of The Vicar of Dibley.

[Although loving Dawn French in lots of other things]

Fly, on the other hand,
spent Christmas with
his family.

Also, Anna Ford tended
to have the day off
which just added to
Tim's sense of isolation.

At Christmas Tim the Tiny Horse
cooked a chicken nugget which
he ate part of hot for Lunch...

then the rest cold over
the next few days.

pudding was
a fruit pastille.

This year Fly had given
Tim a Christmas cracker.

'A fat lot of good that is!'
thought Tim the Tiny Horse,
looking at the cracker.

Then Tim had an Idea.

He wedged one end of the cracker in the doorway and pulled...

and pulled...

 and pulled.

Until the cracker
snapped.

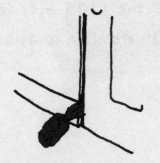

Unfortunately, the d<u>oo</u>r
had won.

Tim the Tiny Horse
was now in a quandary.

Should he take the door's
winnings?

'I'll take the toy
but leave the joke
and hat,'
he thought.

That seemed fair.

The toy was a green plastic horse.

Tim the Tiny Horse sat on the sofa with the green plastic horse and watched...

The Vicar of Dibley.

And for a moment
Tim had an idea of what it
would be like to have a mummy.

(And, on top of that, Dawn French reminded him of a slightly fuller Anna Ford.)

the adventure continues

A lot has happened to
Tim the Tiny Horse since we
last caught up with him.
But if you were hoping that
maybe he'd got bigger...

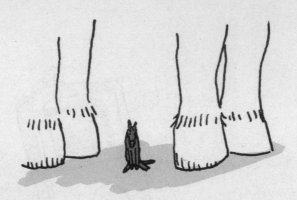

then I'm afraid I must disappoint you. Tim is <u>still</u> a very small horse.

Tim the Tiny Horse

A tic tac

Diagram to show relative size of Tim the Tiny Horse

So small is he in fact that he <u>could</u> use an iPod as his main TV, with the headphones as speakers (his ears are too small to need a sub-woofer) ... but he doesn't.

He is so small that he could
use an acorn cup as a basin,
but chooses not to.

As he doesn't really go for
that Rustic Look.

He is so small that on
one occasion, whilst
eating some spaghetti hoops...

he got one caught over
his nose... and it acted...
as a <u>muzzle</u>!

He had to get
his best friend
(who is a fly)
to bite it off.

Which was a little embarrassing
for both of them.

No, he still cuts a diminutive
figure around the town or
more commonly...

in his matchbox home.

Fly Gets Married

One day Tim's best friend Fly
called to say that he had
important news.

'Fire away!' said Tim.

'No, this is not the sort of news
I can tell you over the phone...'
said Fly.

'I'll be over in five minutes.'

'Hmm,' thought Tim
the Tiny Horse...

'I wonder what Fly's news is?'

Perhaps he'd bought Tim
a present.

No, it wasn't Tim's birthday
for another month.

Bits of 'scratchy'

Perhaps Fly had come into some money and wanted to share his good fortune with Tim.

Tim immediately thought about what he would buy with his share...

and quickly settled on a fudge bar.

That would be <u>More</u> than enough.

He didn't want to be

GREEDY.

Fly didn't actually say
he had g<u>oo</u>d news though...

just ⁞IMPORTANT⁞ news.

maybe that's why
Fly hadn't felt able
to tell Tim the news...

over the phone.

Maybe Fly was
in some sort of
TROUBLE!

He was a bit of a
hot-head.

Maybe he was in a dispute
with a wasp over some
leftover food...

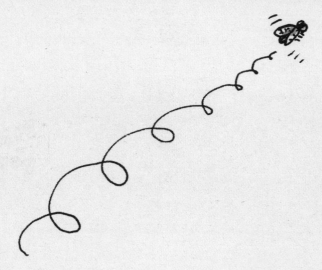

and was having to leave
town for a while to
allow things to cool off.

DING!
DONG!

Just then, the doorbell rang.

It was Fly.

'I'm getting married!'
said Fly.

Tim pulled a face...*

He was really pleased
for Fly ...

*In fact, a series of faces.

but at the same time
was a little concerned.

After all Fly had only known
his girlfriend for a week.

This anxiety swirled around
in Tim's head...

as he thought about how
to react to the news.

Before he knew it, several seconds had passed.

'GREAT!'

Said Tim the Tiny Horse rather half-heartedly.

GREAT!

Unfortunately the pause...

and the face...

and the level of heartedness...

🕐 + 🐴 + 💗 = ?

had said it all.

Tim the Tiny Horse Falls in Love

Tim the Tiny Horse <u>was</u> tiny.
To give you some idea he
was so small that every now
and then he'd stand on
an ice cube...

Grrrr!

and pretend to be
a polar bear.

Small of body, yes...

but oh so big-hearted!

A heart so big that it longed...

nay, yearned ...

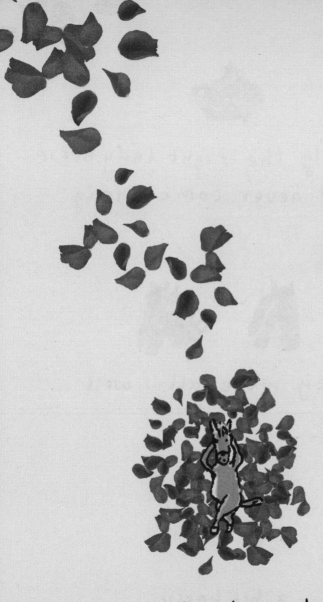

to be loved.

Sadly the right lady horse
had never come along.

They were all ... well ...

a bit bossy ...

and frankly far too big...

During the planning of Fly's wedding Tim had to meet regularly with other members of Fly's family.

Including Fly's sister, Chenille.

Now although Tim had known Chenille for some time he had never really <u>noticed</u> her...

if you know what I mean.

Now he found himself staring
at her, and what's more ...

she appeared to stare back.

This brought on feelings that Tim didn't really understand —

Pumping chest out

Holding tummy in

his heart raced – indeed, galloped...

over hedges and fences.

His face went all red! *

* which on top of his natural blue
colour made purple which made
him look like he was choking
on something.

Tim the Tiny Horse couldn't sleep at night...

for thinking about Fly's sister.

'This must be LOVE,'
thought Tim the Tiny Horse.
And he immediately determined
to tell Chenille of his feelings
for her.

So, the next day, armed with a
forget-me-not, Tim the Tiny Horse
set off for Fly's house to ask
his sister out.

Unfortunately <u>Fly</u> answered the door.

'Is your sister in?' asked Tim.

'Um... I think so...' said Fly,
a little confused.

Fly went and got his sister.

'This is for you,' said
Tim the Tiny Horse,
giving Chenille the
forget-me-not.

'I wondered
whether you'd like
to go for a picnic
sometime?'

'No ta!' said
Chenille, handing the
flower right back to Tim.

This Stumped Tim for a moment.

'It was just... that I noticed the way you looked at me,' he continued.

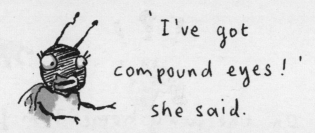

'I've got
compound eyes!'
she said.

'All us flies do, I look at
everything all the time,
don't read anything into
that!'

It seemed he had totally
misread the situation.

On the way home Tim felt rather sad.

Then he thought about the racing heart...

the purple face...

<u>and</u> that he'd never actually
heard of a horse marrying a
fly before.

'Oh well, better to have loved and lost!' thought Tim the Tiny Horse, and that night...

he slept like a log.

Tim's Best
Friend's Wedding

After Tim had got over the initial
shock of Fly's marriage plans—

(Fly had explained that because flies only tended to live about a year, in fact a week's courtship was perfectly respectable.

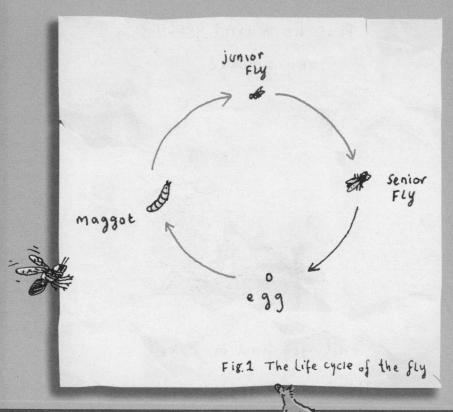

Fig.1 The life cycle of the fly

Plus he wasn't getting
any younger...

and you had to take
your opportunities where
you could.)

— Tim had some consolation from Fly asking him to be 'Best Horse'.

Tim took this as the ultimate endorsement of their friendship.

'What exactly
does it entail?'

Said Tim the Tiny
Horse.*

'There are various duties,'
said Fly. 'But the main one
is the Best Man's Speech!'

* He liked using the word tail
  in words.

Tim was so anxious at the thought of this...

that he staggered back...

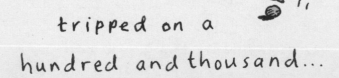

tripped on a
hundred and thousand...

 ...and landed in
Fly's grandma's lap.

(Fly's grandma was now living
with Fly as she was unable to
cope on her own and was a risk
to herself from spiders.)

chair lift

Big hairy
spider

'A speech! Quelle horreur!'
he thought, lapsing into French.

'Yes, it should be funny too,'
said Fly. 'But keep it <u>clean</u>.'

On the way home he bought a book called '101 Jokes For Your Best Man's Speech' by someone called Barry Cryer.

'Funny name for a comedian,' thought Tim the Tiny Horse.

As he read through it Tim realised
that whilst being very funny some
of the jokes were rather rude.

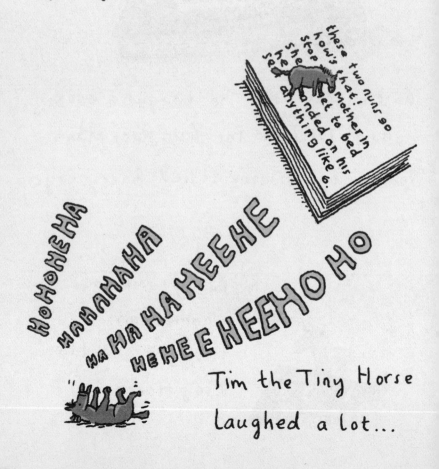

these two nuns go
how's that!
stop
get to bed
she
he
landed on his
said
anything like o.

HOHOHEHA
HAHAHAHA
HAHAHAHEEHE
HEHEE HEEHO HO

"

Tim the Tiny Horse
laughed a lot...

but had a vision
of Fly's grandma

having a setback
if she ever heard them.

'You're on your own on this one,'
he thought to himself.

But he just couldn't think
of anything funny to say.

So he just wrote about why
he liked Fly and what
a good friend he was.

On the big day the speech went down a storm.

Many of the guests had tears in their eyes.

In fact it went down so well that Tim decided to sling in one of the jokes from the book...

(a particularly saucy one involving an actress, a bishop... and a goat)

HA HA-OOPS!

and Fly's grandma laughed so hard she fell off her chair.

Mr & Mrs Fly Get a New Addition

Tim the Tiny Horse noticed that Fly's new wife had put on a little weight...

and that her breath had
started to smell of pickled
onions.

Well, you didn't have to be
Dr Robert Winston to work
out that this probably meant
that Fly's new wife was
going to have a MAGGOT.

'Indeed she is!'
beamed Fly, proudly.

'Congratulations!'
Said Tim.

Although he _actually_ thought
it was a little soon.

After all they'd only been
married a day and a half.

Tim hadn't even eaten his piece of wedding cake...

and the photos weren't even back from the printer's.

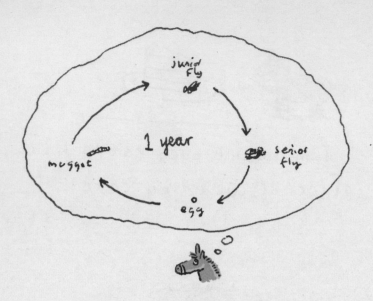

Then Tim remembered
the urgency of the fly's
life cycle...

and let it pass.

Fly and his wife set about
making their home more
baby friendly.

They installed a cot...

bought a number
of soft toys...

and even painted the walls of
the nursery with well-known
fly children's characters
such as...

Mickey Fly...

The
Telly-Flybbies...

and Flyddy
[the little fly...

~~with~~ the red-and-yellow car].

In no time Fly's wife had given birth to a baby fly or 'Maggot'.

'He's got your nose!'
said Tim to Fly.

(closer)
view

{ much
closer view
so you can
see his face }

Everyone stared at Maggot,
who rolled around on his
blanket...

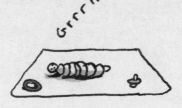

and who made noises...

from both ends.

Tim couldn't really see what this baby had to offer.

Then Maggot looked straight at Tim...

and <u>smiled</u>.

Tim smiled back.

Now he understood.

Tim the Tiny Horse Babysits for Fly

Tim the Tiny Horse felt rather
sorry for Fly and his wife...

the pair of them always
looked <u>so</u> tired.

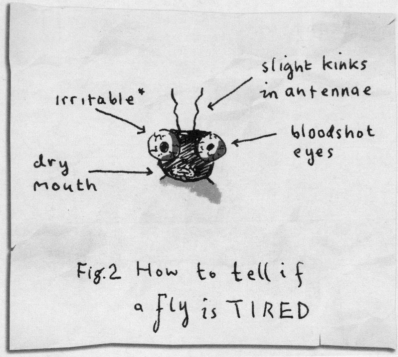

Fig.2 How to tell if
a fly is TIRED

* Always arguing with wife.

So he offered to babysit Maggot
for them so they could have
a night off.

'How about tonight?' said Fly,
grabbing his coat.

'Um... ok,' said Tim,
taken aback slightly by Fly's
keenness.

'See you later!'
        he said ...

but they had already gone.

WAH!
WAH!
WAH!

Straight away, Maggot
woke up and started crying.

[Tim could hear him on the baby listening device.]

So Tim turned the listening
device off.

'That's better,'
thought Tim
the Tiny Horse.

Then he felt a little guilty.

Tim went and got
the screaming Maggot
from his cot...

and walked him up ...

and down.

Pretty soon Maggot was
fast asleep.

Until Tim put him
back in his cot...

at which point
he woke up...

WAH!

and started
screaming again.

Tim wasn't sure...

but this screaming seemed
louder than the last lot.

Tim walked Maggot up and down
again...

but every time he tried
to put Maggot down he
started screaming.

Tim tried everything to
get Maggot off to sleep.

He tried counting
sheep out loud...

but fell asleep himself...

only to be woken
by Maggot's
screaming.

WAH!
WAH!
WAH!

 He tried feeding him...

 Gulp!
Gulp!
Gulp!

and even sang
him a lullaby.

[Being an orphan, Tim didn't
know any lullabies and so had
to make one up.]

Go To Sleep Little Maggot

words & music T.T. Tiny-Horse

Go to sleep little maggot
Please don't cry
Stop that racket I beg of you
And one day you'll be a fly.

Chorus
Oh where are your parents?
Surely they can't be much longer!
It's doing my head in
I'm never having children
If it's like this.

Yes, it wasn't great, but it
did the trick.

SCREAAM!"

Until Tim put Maggot back in his cot.

'Scream!'
bellowed Maggot.

'Sshut up!'
bellowed Tim
the Tiny Horse
(completely blowing his top).

Unfortunately...

Fly and his wife had returned home at this point and were in the front room with the baby listening device.

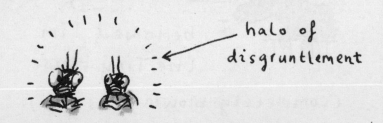

halo of disgruntlement

Tim wasn't employed
as a babysitter again.

And from then on
Maggot always eyed
him with some suspicion.

'It's probably for the best,'
thought Tim the Tiny Horse.

'After all...'

' know your strengths. '

tim
gets a pet

With Fly now a family man...

Tim found that he had a bit more time on his hands.

And when there was nothing on the box he would feel...

bored ...

Or worse — lonely.

[but never sorry for himself — he was just putting that sad face on for the picture.]

One bank holiday monday, whilst taking a stroll he saw a man walking his dog.

'Humans have pets for company!' he thought.

'That is exactly what I should do!'

... and he headed off
to the pet shop.

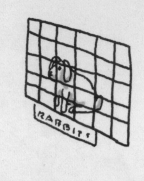

Unfortunately all the pets in the shop were rather too big. Some of them were downright frightening.

GRRrr!

AARRrr!

Especially the dogs.

Even the hamsters were
the size of elephants to
Tim the Tiny Horse.

PETS 'R' US

'Ho-Hum,' thought Tim the Tiny Horse.

'It looks like I must settle for a life on my own.'

Just then, he spotted a greenfly snacking on the stem of a flower.

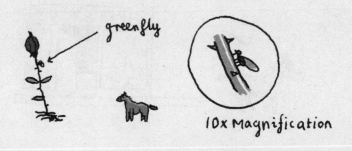

greenfly

10x Magnification

Tim got chatting to the greenfly
(who didn't seem to be that bright).

vacant-looking eyes

'I don't suppose you'd be my pet?'
asked Tim the Tiny Horse.

'Sure, why not?' said the
greenfly.

'Great!' said Tim.
'What's your name?'

'George!'
said the greenfly.

And with that, using a piece
of cotton as a lead, Tim
took his new pet home.

tim and george get to know each other better

It turned out that Tim the Tiny Horse and George the Greenfly had quite different tastes.

Tim liked to eat
Hula Hoops and
sugar lumps...

whilst George liked to
drink <u>SAP</u>.

Tim liked to play swingball...

whilst George liked to
drink SAP.

Tim had an interest in current affairs...

whilst George liked to watch 'Emmerdale'...

whilst drinking SAP.

As alluded to earlier, George didn't seem to have a articularly high IQ.

'What's that?' said George, pointing up at the sky.

'It's the sky,'
answered Tim.

'Big, isn't it?'
said George.

'Well spotted,' said Tim,
a hint of sarcasm creeping
into his voice.

'what's the sky for?'
asked George the Greenfly.

'Um... it provides us
with <u>air</u>,' said Tim,
hopefully.

'What's air?'
asked George.

'Is that some <u>SAP</u> I can see
over there by that bush?'
said Tim the Tiny Horse.

And George bounded over to
the bush to investigate.

mmm....sap!

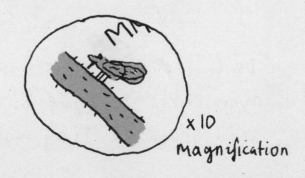

x10
magnification

On George's first night at
Tim's house, Tim had made
him a bed from four bobbles
off a jumper.

But every time Tim put George
into his bed George would climb
up...

on to the end of Tim's bed.

If Tim returned George

to his bed...

out he would pop.

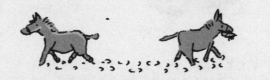

After five of these episodes...

Tim gave up.

'This pet lark is proving
to be quite a strain,'
he thought.

He looked down at George
asleep on the end of his
bed and had to admit...

he was already quite
fond of him.

'A greenfly is for life...
not just for bank holiday
Monday.'

Tim the Tiny Horse had never
had much in the way of
material goods.

So imagine his excitement when he received a cheque for a considerable sum of money from sales of his book.

'I should be careful with this money,' thought Tim the Tiny Horse.

'This sort of luck
doesn't come along
every day...'

'I should invest it...

...in a buy-to-let flat!'

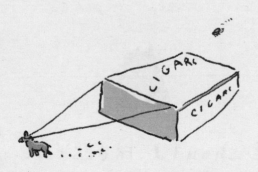

He went straight out and bought
himself an empty cigar box...

and set about converting it
into a 'Loft-Style' apartment.

He'd learnt from the TV
that it was important to
keep things neutral.

So he painted the inside
of the box with
Tipp-Ex.

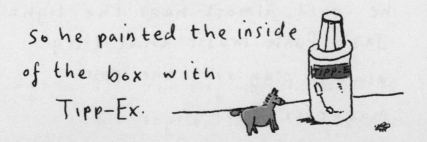

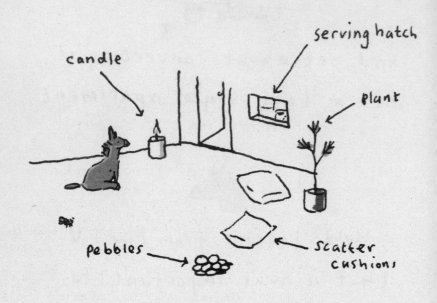

candle

serving hatch

plant

pebbles

scatter cushions

As he surveyed his handiwork he could almost hear the light, jazz-funk music that they always play over the post-makeover footage.

'I won't have any problem
shifting this,' he thought.

Within a couple
of days a ladybird turned up;
it seemed her own house had
burnt down.

'Is that a greenfly?'
said the ladybird,
looking at George...

and licking her lips.

'Yes, but you wouldn't
want to eat him... he's ill,'
lied Tim. 'Listen, take
the flat rent-free until
you're back on your feet,'
he said, taking pity on
the ladybird.

So, not only had he spent
a lot of money on the refurb
[Tipp-Ex isn't cheap, you know] ...

he now wasn't getting any
money in to cover his costs.

A couple of weeks later
Tim the Tiny Horse received
a complaint from the
neighbours ...

that the ladybird had had
rather too many guests...

many of whom
had stayed overnight.

when he went to visit
the property...

he found fifteen
juvenile ants living there!

Inside there was utter chaos!

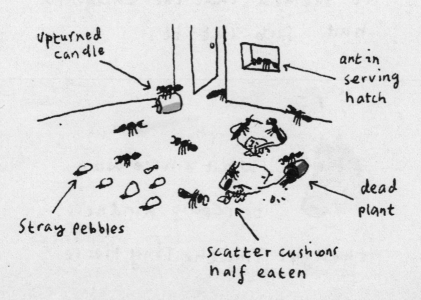

upturned
candle

ant in
serving
hatch

dead
plant

Stray pebbles

scatter cushions
half eaten

It seemed that the Ladybird had sub-let it.

'What a nice way to repay kindness!'

thought Tim the Tiny Horse.

With the help of Fly and a trail of sugar, Tim managed to get the ants to leave his cigar-box apartment.

Tim's experiences in the property market had been something of a <u>let-down</u>.

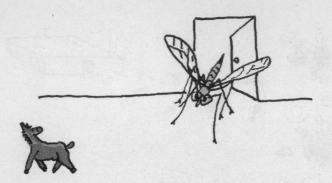

So he flogged the flat to
a daddy long legs.

Sometimes it's just nice to
know your money's safe.

tim & george go to the park

Every now and then
Tim the Tiny Horse would take his
pet greenfly George to the park...

for a run around.

To say George was lazy
Would be unkind....

but true.

In fact if there was any
running around to be done...

It was usually done by Tim.

Sometimes Tim and Fly would play
'Piggy in the Middle' with George.

But George would just sit
there...

dreaming of sap.

Tim tried throwing sticks for George

George would amble over to the

stick...

... and try to suck any remaining
sap from it.

One day Tim threw a stick for
George which landed in...

a bush.

Off George ambled, whilst Tim sat
back and soaked up the sun.

Tim nodded off.

Only to wake up 8 minutes later.

He looked around, but there
was no sign of George.

'George!' he called, 'Get back here right now!'

He ran into the bush.

And there was George, cornered by
the very same ladybird that Tim had
rented his flat to!

gnash!
gnash!

She had a wild look in her eye
and was gnashing her mandibles
in a most alarming way.

...And there was poor George.

Tim reared up to his full height
(about 1 centimetre)...

and let out the loudest 'neigh'
he could.

The ladybird hesitated
for a moment...

Tutted...

'tut!'

spread her wings...

and flew off.

'That was a close one'
said Tim to George.

'I think we have found
an <u>arch</u>-<u>enemy</u>.'

When they got home, Tim
gave George a grape as
a treat.

which he made short work of.

Then they both had
an early night.

tim gets wet

One day Tim threw a particularly
juicy stick for George...

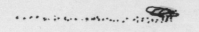

which landed in a puddle.

But instead of stopping at
the water's edge...

George dived into the puddle

and disappeared under the
water.

Tim waited for George to
           re-surface...

but there was no sign
of the little greenfly

except for one bubble.

Tim suddenly remembered
that on the whole greenflies
can't swim

(as anyone who drinks tea will tell you)

Quick as a flash Tim took off
his shoes...

and dived into the puddle.

It was a very deep puddle.

Tim splashed about gasping
for air...

Then he remembered that
he couldn't swim either!

Under the water he went...

then he managed to grab at
a length of cotton floating on
the water's surface.

As he took hold of the cotton
he found he was being dragged
to shore.

where he found that the piece
of cotton was being pulled by
George the Greenfly.

'You're a bit wet!'
said George.

'Hm!' said Tim the Tiny Horse.

tim thinks about selling out

Tim

a Tic-Tac

Tim the Tiny Horse was <u>tiny</u>.

BORDERSTONES

but since he was now a published
author he was in demand.

Why, he'd even been interviewed by
top TV presenter Mariella Frostrup.

He tried not to let this extra attention go to his head.

but if he was honest...
every now and then...

wazzup?

it did. For instance...

Once he'd been waiting so long
at the Deli counter in the
supermarket...

that he bellowed at the top of
his voice:

Fortunately, no one could hear him (because he was so small)

Tim now bought his olives on the internet.

One day Tim had a phone call
from a lady asking if he'd
like to be in an advert

'Absolutely not!' Thought
Tim the Tiny Horse

'I would never compromise
my artistic integrity

by saying something I didn't
mean, for money!'

Then the lady told him
the fee.

'Send the script over
and I'll think about it,'
said Tim, hedging his bets.

Unfortunately the advert
was for FLY SPRAY.

Which put Tim in a rather tricky predicament.

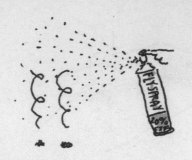

Should he promote something that might well be used to kill his best friend and his pet?*

No contest. He turned the advert down.

---

*A problem peculiar to those who consort with insects.

Imagine his disgust when 2 months later he caught the same advert on TV featuring

His arch-enemy the <u>lady</u><u>bird</u> in a blue horse costume.

It was becoming clear that
ladybirds had absolutely
no sense of fair play.

tim loses george

One morning when Tim the Tiny
Horse took George the Greenfly
his usual bowl of sap he
didn't stir.

When the bowl was
still full of sap at lunchtime...

Tim started to get a little
concerned.

George was very still...

and nothing Tim did...

would wake him up.

Tim called the vet, who quickly worked out that George the Greenfly had, in fact...

died.

'I'm afraid he's dead,' said
the vet...

and handed Tim a rather
large bill.

Tim was very upset...

not just at the bill...

but at losing his trusted
(sort of) pet.

Tim tried to cheer himself up
by imagining George in heaven...

fluttering about...

and drinking as much sap
as he wanted.

mmm...sap!

There was a small funeral for
George. All Fly's family came
(even Chenille).

Fly's mum sang 'The circle of Life'... which was one of George's favourites.

Tim found there were advantages to not being a pet owner again.

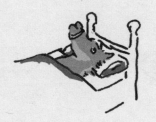

For instance, Tim didn't have to worry about taking George out for walks...

or keeping the larder
stocked with fresh supplies
of sap.

But whilst George wasn't
the world's greatest
conversationalist...

and had rather narrow
interests (i.e. sap)...

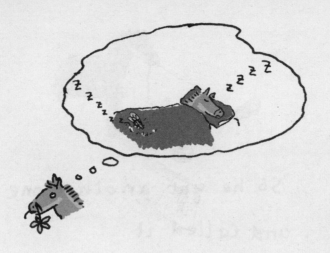

he had a certain <u>presence</u>...

and Tim missed the little
greenfly very much.

So he got another one
and called it . . .

George the Second!

The end

Also available: